T0054259

POCKET POWER
from
THE SLUMFLOWER

CHIDERA EGGERUE

**KNOW YOUR WORTH
AND ACT ON IT**

Hardie Grant

QUADRILLE

INTRODUCTION

This book is dedicated to the women who love too much and leave nothing for themselves.

Sometimes, we overcomplicate and overthink what it means to stand in our power – especially when we date men. Life is not a magical fairytale where people automatically treat you wonderfully just because you are a nice person. You have to demand what you deserve, babe! Men aren't going to magically and effortlessly give you the treatment you deserve – especially if they perceive you to be a pushover. That's life under patriarchy.

I've learnt that if you act like a doormat, men will almost always take the opportunity to trample you. But if you act like a woman with standards, boundaries and clear communication about what makes you feel good, the men who are meant for you will endeavour to enhance your pleasure and wellbeing. Men will never be perfect but in this life, you get what you advocate for.

This is your only life. Accept that you will get things wrong on this journey. There will be men you will mess up with by giving them too much – whether that's too much of an emotional response, too much attention or too many chances. That's okay. Grow with what you know and move on. Take the lesson, charge it to the game and remain focused on having more self control, patience and trust in yourself to evaluate properly next time. Don't forget to be kind to yourself. You've got this!

JUST BECAUSE YOU LIKE HIM DOESN'T MEAN YOU NEED TO MAKE HIM THE EXCEPTION.

HE NEEDS TO MAKE HIMSELF EXCEPTIONAL.

IF HE'S
A FEEDER,

HE'S A
PLEASER.

YOU WATER WHAT YOU
WANT TO GROW.

STATUS DOESN'T NECESSARILY GRANT SELF ESTEEM.

YOU STILL HAVE TO WORK FOR THAT.

THERE ARE NO REWARDS FOR BEING 'THE NICE GIRL'.

JUST RESENTMENT FOR NOT RECEIVING THE RECIPROCATION YOU DESERVED.

OPPRESSED PEOPLE DON'T HAVE TO RESPOND NICELY TO OPPRESSION.

WE SHOULD ALL BE ASKING WHY
THERE IS OPPRESSION TO BE
RESPONDING TO IN THE FIRST PLACE,
NOT POLICING THE WAY PEOPLE
RESPOND TO OPPRESSION.

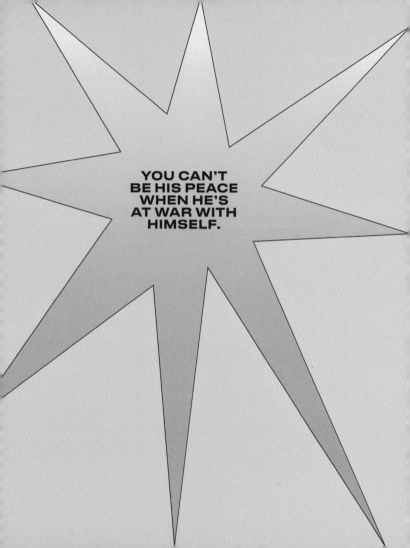

YOU CAN'T
BE HIS PEACE
WHEN HE'S
AT WAR WITH
HIMSELF.

HONOUR YOURSELF AND LEAVE WHEN YOU'VE TRULY HAD ENOUGH; YOU CAN'T STAY AND BE COMPLAINING.

THAT'S LIKE LICKING
THE PLATE CLEAN
AND SAYING YOU DIDN'T
ENJOY THE FOOD.

PUT THE TOOLBOX DOWN FOR A SECOND AND LET'S TALK:

IF YOU COLLATE ALL THE HOURS
IN YOUR LIFE THAT YOU HAVE SPENT
ON FIXING MEN, HOW DIFFERENT
WOULD YOUR LIFE LOOK IF THAT TIME
WAS INSTEAD, SPENT ON YOU?

WHEN YOU HURT SOMEONE, YOU DON'T GET TO DECIDE WHICH VERSION OF YOU THEY REMEMBER.

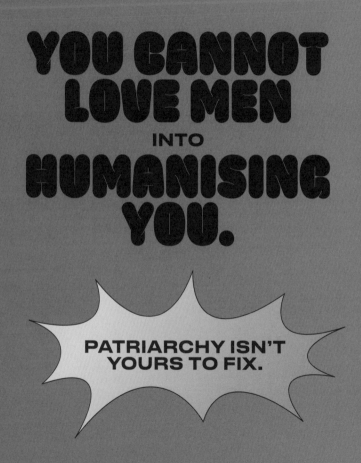

IF THEY COME BACK EXACTLY
AS THEY WERE, LEAVE THEM
EXACTLY AS THEY CAME.

JUST BECAUSE HE
MISSES YOU, IT DOESN'T
MEAN HE'S CHANGED.

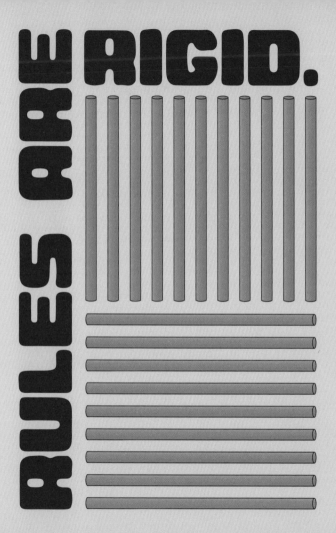

RULES ARE RIGID.

PRINCIPLES ALLOW YOU TO PIVOT AROUND YOUR VALUES.

LET YOUR PRINCIPLES FORM THE FOUNDATION OF ANY DECISION YOU MAKE BECAUSE THEY REST ON YOUR CORE VALUES AS A HUMAN BEING.

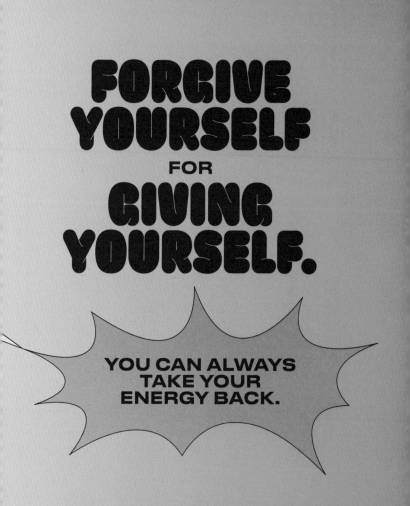

IF MEN VALUED WOMEN
THE WAY THEY VALUED
HAVING SEX WITH US,

WHAT WOULD THE

WORLD LOOK LIKE?

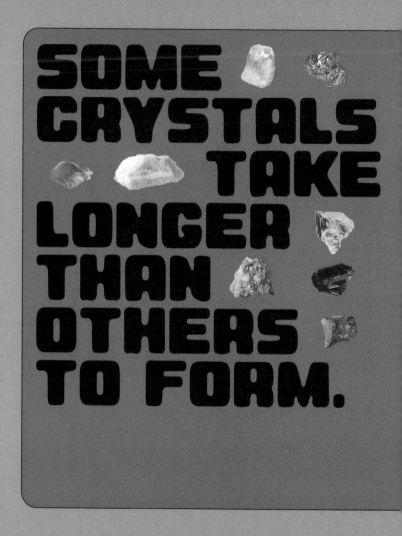

SOME CRYSTALS TAKE LONGER THAN OTHERS TO FORM.

I TRUST THAT MY PROCESS WILL BE WORTH IT.

TRUST YOURSELF ENOUGH TO DO IT YOUR WAY WHETHER THAT'S

DATING,
OR DECO

DANCING.
RATING.

IF
'THAT'S
JUST
HOW
HE
IS',
THEN
THAT'S
WHO
HE
IS,

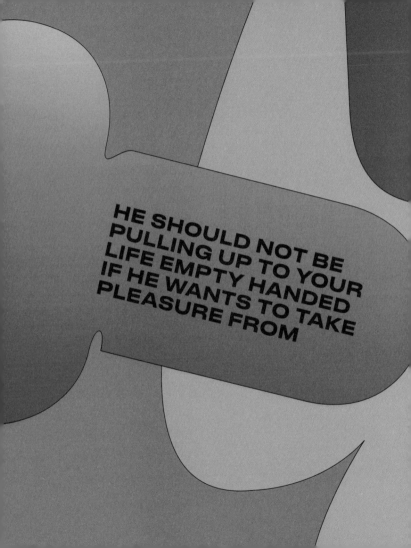

HE SHOULD NOT BE
PULLING UP TO YOUR
LIFE EMPTY HANDED
IF HE WANTS TO TAKE
PLEASURE FROM

IF HIS DESIRE TO BE RIGHT
IS MORE IMPORTANT THAN HIS
DESIRE TO TREAT YOU RIGHT,

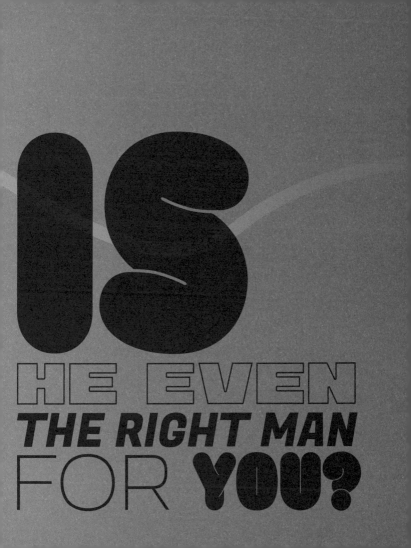

IS

HE EVEN

THE RIGHT MAN

FOR **YOU?**

SOMETIMES YOU MAY HAVE TO SACRIFICE THE CONNECTION YOU'RE ENJOYING IN ORDER TO SET A STANDARD...

AND IF THIS STANDARD COMES AT THE EXPENSE OF YOUR 'CONNECTION', DID IT EVER REALLY EXIST TO BEGIN WITH?

UNDER PATRIARCHY, MEN DEPEND ON YOUR FIXATION WITH BEING A 'GOOD PERSON' BECAUSE IT DISTRACTS YOU FROM

BEING AN AUTHENTIC HUMAN BEING, WHO IS SIMPLY HAVING A REASONABLE RESPONSE TO OPPRESSION.

NICE GIRL SYNDROME GOTTA GO, 'CAUSE IF IT WORKS, IT WOULD HAVE WORKED BY NOW.

SO WHAT'S NEXT?

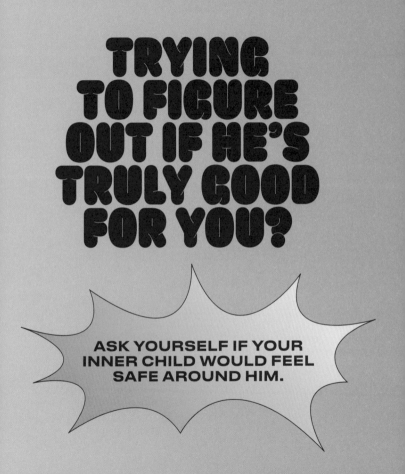

DATING A MAN WHO DOESN'T WANT TO INVEST IN YOU IS LIKE CARRYING HEAVY SHOPPING BAGS

WHILST A MAN WALKS ALONGSIDE YOU EMPTY-HANDED.

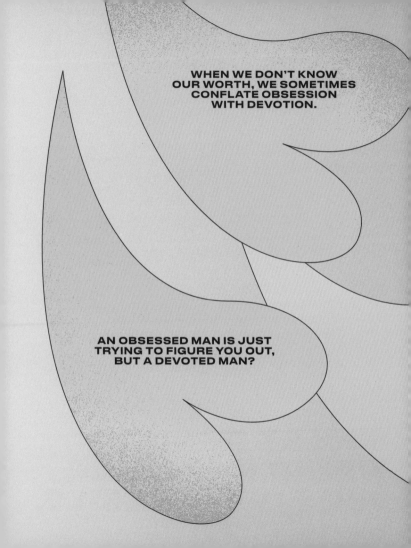

WHEN WE DON'T KNOW
OUR WORTH, WE SOMETIMES
CONFLATE OBSESSION
WITH DEVOTION.

AN OBSESSED MAN IS JUST
TRYING TO FIGURE YOU OUT,
BUT A DEVOTED MAN?

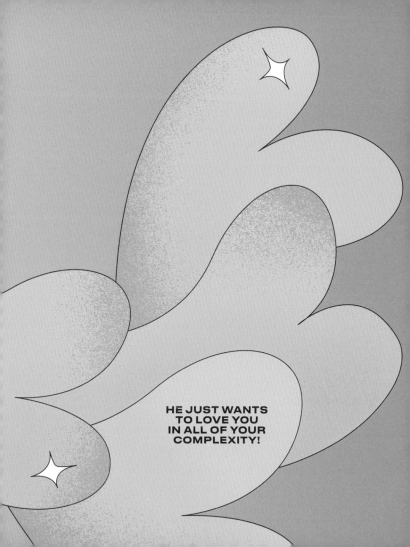

THE TIME WILL PASS ANYWAY!
WHAT WILL YOU DO WHILE THAT
TIME PASSES?

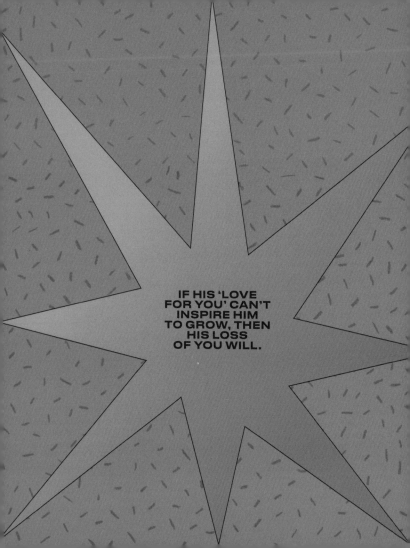

IF HIS 'LOVE
FOR YOU' CAN'T
INSPIRE HIM
TO GROW, THEN
HIS LOSS
OF YOU WILL.

RADICAL EMPATHY FOR SELF.

FUCK EVERYTHING ELSE.

A HARD-WORKING WOMAN
DESERVES A MAN WHO WORKS
HARD FOR HER HAPPINESS.

THE DAY YOU FINALLY DECIDE YOU'VE HAD ENOUGH, WILL BE THE MOST IMPORTANT DAY OF YOUR LIFE.

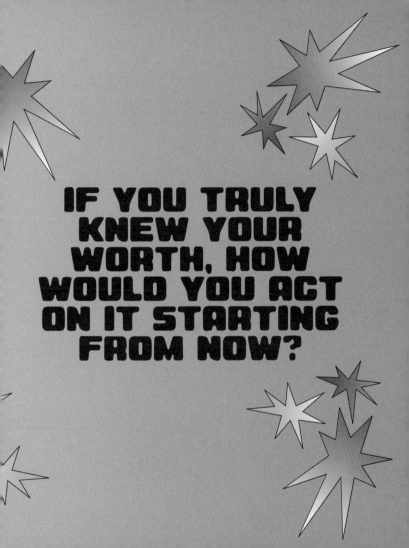

IF YOU'RE IN A PLACE WHERE YOU HAVE A FRAGILE ATTACHMENT TO MEN'S OPINIONS OF YOU, MAYBE YOU AREN'T YET READY TO DATE AND

INSTEAD, IT MIGHT BE TIME FOR A BREAK BUT NOT BEING READY TO DATE DOES NOT MEAN YOU ARE NOT READY TO BE LOVED!

WHEN IT COMES TO DECIDING WHICH MEN DESERVE SPACE IN YOUR LIFE,

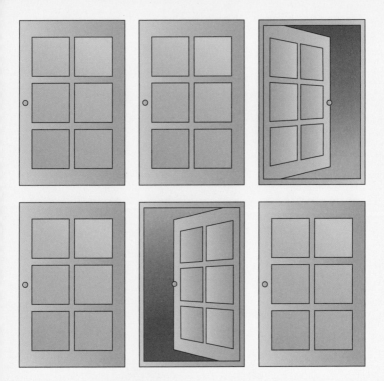

MOST GUYS WON'T MAKE THE CUT AND YOU HAVE TO ACCEPT AND TRUST YOUR OBSERVATIONS – NO MATTER HOW BADLY YOU MAY WANT TO BELIEVE OTHERWISE.

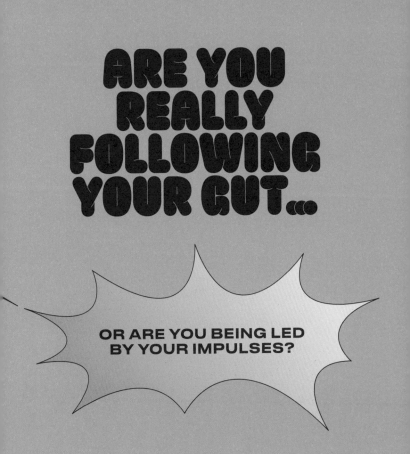

IS YOUR SEARCH FOR ROMANTIC
DOPAMINE FUELLING YOUR
DESPERATION AND THUS,

LEADING YOU
DISAPPO

TO MORE
ITMENT?

THERE IS A VERSION OF YOU THAT
KNOWS HOW TO USE YOUR IMPULSES
TO YOUR ADVANTAGE - AS OPPOSED
TO ALWAYS GIVING INTO URGES YOU
HAVEN'T CONFRONTED.

WHAT STEPS WILL YOU TAKE TO MERGE WITH HER?

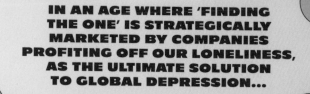

IN AN AGE WHERE 'FINDING THE ONE' IS STRATEGICALLY MARKETED BY COMPANIES PROFITING OFF OUR LONELINESS, AS THE ULTIMATE SOLUTION TO GLOBAL DEPRESSION...

TWO THINGS CAN BE TRUE AT ONCE:
I FANCY THIS GUY BECAUSE HE'S FUNNY
AND HOT, BUT I ALSO ACKNOWLEDGE
THAT HE CANNOT MEET MY NEEDS NOR
CREATE THE FEELINGS I DESIRE IN DATING -

AND AS A RESULT OF SUCH OBSERVATION,
I WILL FOCUS ON PUTTING MYSELF FIRST
INSTEAD OF GIVING INTO THE URGE OF
ACTING ON MY SUPERFICIAL ATTRACTION.

WELL, SIMILARLY, DON'T DATE WHEN YOU'RE DESPERATE BECAUSE YOU'RE MORE LIKELY TO END UP WITH A MAN WHO WILL STARVE YOUR SOUL AND FEED YOUR EGO!

IF YOU DON'T RECOGNISE YOUR WORTH,

SOMEONE ELSE WILL DECIDE IT FOR YOU.

SO LIKE CLOCKWORK, IT FINALLY
HAPPENED: HE CAME BACK AFTER
WASTING YOUR TIME...

ARE YOU GOING TO FALL FOR IT AGAIN THIS TIME, OR ARE YOU GOING TO FOCUS ON YOURSELF?

LIKE AN UNSOLICITED
MAILING LIST SUBSCRIPTION,
YOU HAVE THE RIGHT TO OPT
OUT OF A MAN'S PROBLEMS.
THERE'S NO PERFECT MAN
BUT THERE ARE MEN WHO ARE
MEANT FOR YOU.

IF AFTER ALL HIS FLIRTING
AND FONDLING HE'S SUDDENLY
DEVELOPED COLD FEET,
LEAVE HIM IN THE COLD.
HE WILL BE FINE.

DON'T LAY WITH MEN WHO WON'T

LIFT

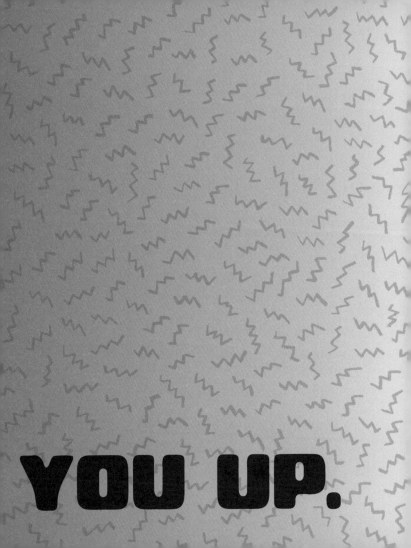

INTEGRITY IS EXPENSIVE BUT IT ALWAYS PAYS OFF.

ACKNOWLEDGEMENTS

This book is dedicated to the friends in my life who lifted me up when the world got too heavy for me. To Hussain Manawer, thank you for the years of endless walks we'd go on together – even if I was sad and needed you at 11pm. To Natasha Boyce, I am grateful for the soft space you've held for me, and all the times you would end our phone calls with 'Girl, we need a quote book from you!' This book exists because of you. And to Georgina Wahed, thank you for being a friend and a fighter for me behind the scenes. I'm grateful to know your sweet lion spirit!

ABOUT THE AUTHOR

Chidera Eggerue, popularly known as The Slumflower, is an author and advocate who rose to popularity with her viral movement #saggyboobsmatter in 2018. Chidera's debut book *What a Time To Be Alone* has since become a *Sunday Times* No. 1 Bestseller and she has continued to bring feminist issues to the fore, including through her 2020 Channel 4 documentary *Bring Back the Bush* and her 2021 appearance in the BBC2 documentary *Womanhood*, where she starred next to prominent women such as Shirley Ballas and Sinitta. She spoke in support of sex work and feminism at Cambridge University in 2022, and 2023 saw the release of her much-awaited podcast 'The Slumflower Hour', through which Chidera has created a 'domain for disobedient women who date men'. Chidera remains adamant about using her platform to encourage an image of Black women that doesn't involve playing by the rules.

Managing Director: Sarah Lavelle
Head of Design: Claire Rochford
Design and Illustration: Evi-O.Studio | Katherine Zhang
Head of Production: Stephen Lang
Production Controller: Sabeena Atchia

Published in 2023 by Quadrille,
an imprint of Hardie Grant Publishing

Quadrille
52–54 Southwark Street
London SE1 1UN
quadrille.com

Cataloguing in Publication Data: a catalogue record
for this book is available from the British Library.

ISBN 978 1 83783 132 6

Printed in China

MIX
Paper | Supporting
responsible forestry
FSC™ C020056